PRAIRIES

DOROTHY HINSHAW PATENT

photographs by

WILLIAM MUÑOZ

Holiday House/New York

Text copyright © 1996 by Dorothy Hinshaw Patent
Photographs copyright © 1996 by William Muñoz
All rights reserved
Printed in the United States of America
First Edition

Library of Congress Cataloging-in-Publication Data
Patent, Dorothy Hinshaw.
Prairies/Dorothy Hinshaw Patent; photographs by William Muñoz.
— 1st ed.
p.   cm.
Includes index.
Summary: Describes the characteristics of the North American
prairie, the plants and animals found there, and the efforts made to
preserve and restore the landscape that once stretched unbroken from
southern Canada into northernmost Mexico.
ISBN 0-8234-1277-6 (hardcover: alk. paper)
1. Prairies — United States — Juvenile literature.   2. Prairie
ecology — United States — Juvenile literature.   3. Prairie
conservation — United States — Juvenile literature.   [1. Prairies.
2. Prairie ecology.   3. Ecology.]   I. Muñoz, William, ill.
II. Title.
QH87.7.P38   1996   96-14125   CIP   AC
574.5′2643′0973 — dc20

Contents

Chapter One   The American Prairie   7

Chapter Two   Prairie Plants   12

Chapter Three Animals of the Prairie   20

Chapter Four   The Destruction of the Prairie   28

Chapter Five   Bringing Back the Prairie   34

               Glossary   39

               Index   40

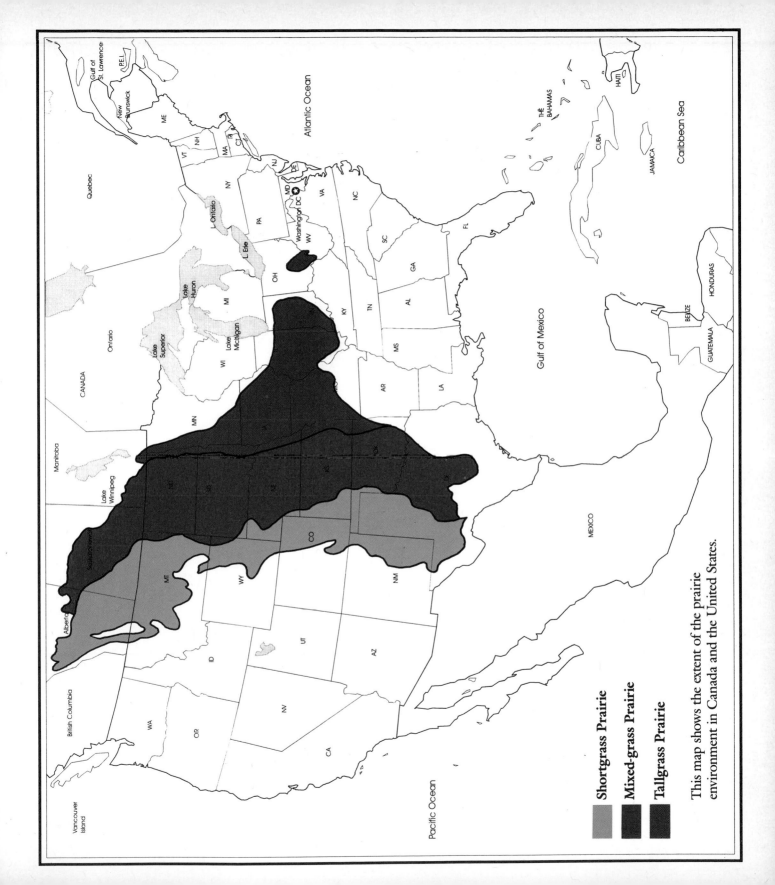

Shortgrass Prairie

Mixed-grass Prairie

Tallgrass Prairie

This map shows the extent of the prairie environment in Canada and the United States.

The open prairie has a beauty that is all its own.

CHAPTER ONE

The American Prairie

Think about grass, the grass of a meadow. Meadow grass is different from lawn grass. A lawn is kept green and short, with just a few other plants growing in it. A meadow is green only in the spring. For much of the rest of the year, it is brown. Its grass is at least a foot tall, sometimes taller. Now picture a meadow all around you, stretching as far as you can see. No matter which way you turn, all you can see is meadow, with blue sky above the horizon. You see no houses, no trees, no streams, no ponds. That's what a prairie looks like.

The American prairie was once a vast grassland that stretched thousands of miles through the middle of the continent, from southern Canada into northernmost Mexico. Even though most of the wild prairie is gone today, people still refer to the region as the "prairie states" and the "prairie provinces."

To the east of the prairie is forest. To the west are the Rocky Mountains. Why does prairie grow between the mountains and the forest? Prairie bridges this gap because of the pattern of rainfall. Weather systems in western North America usually move from west to east. When they hit the Rocky Mountains, the moisture comes out as rain or snow. So, after crossing the Rockies, the moisture has been reduced and the air carries little water. Across the prairies, rainfall is too sparse to support forests—only 10 to 30 inches of rain a year falls on the grasslands.

The Rocky Mountains, seen in the distance, extract moisture from the clouds as rain, producing the prairie.

Storm clouds are impressive over the prairie.

Once, the grasslands were wild. To the west, where the least rain falls, lived tough shortgrass that could survive drought. Now, most of that wild shortgrass is gone.

The eastern prairies receive more rain than those farther west. As the dry western air from which the Rockies took out the moisture moves over the plains, new moist air flowing up from the Gulf of Mexico joins it. This added moisture can come out as rain. Taller grasses that need more water can grow on the wetter eastern prairie. Some are taller than the back of a horse.

There is no visible dividing line between tall- and short-grass prairie. Instead, a mixed-grass area spreads between them. Just where one type begins and ends depends on the landscape and the recent rainfall history.

Fire helps maintain and nourish prairies.

Wind and fire are also important elements of the prairie. Because no natural barriers exist on prairies, the wind can blow and blow and blow, rippling the grass in waves that have a life of their own. The combination of wind and dryness leads to fire. Thunderstorms on the prairie can be violent, with lightning sparking fires that race for miles on the wind. The fires help maintain the prairie, killing invading young trees. The tops of prairie plants are consumed by the fire. But the roots and seeds survive and grow, nourished by nutrients released from the burned-up dead tops.

Before European settlers came, the prairies were the home of Native Americans who had a hand in maintaining them through setting fires. Abundant wildlife lived there, too. Bison, also called buffalo, are prairie creatures. But the elk, grizzly bears, and wolves that we associate with forests also once lived on the prairie. Because we destroyed and took over most of their original homelands, these creatures retreated into the forests and mountains.

Bison, also called buffalo, are native to the prairie.

CHAPTER TWO

Prairie Plants

Grasses are the most obvious prairie plants. Shortgrasses grow up to 2 feet (61 centimeters) tall, while tallgrasses can reach more than 5 feet (152 centimeters). On the mixed-grass prairie, some areas have tallgrasses, some shortgrasses, and others have species growing 2 to 4 feet (61 to 122 centimeters) tall.

Grasses are one of the most successful kinds of plants on earth. They form the third largest family of flowering plants and have more species found worldwide than any other plant family.

A quarter of the earth's land is covered by grasses. Antarctica is the only continent without grasslands. In Asia, the grasslands are called the steppes. The pampas are the South American grasslands, while in South Africa, grasslands are called the veldt.

Tallgrass stretches up toward the sky.

Field corn is a major crop, grown where tall-grass prairie once flourished.

You may not think of eating grass. But grasses feed more people than any other kind of plant. Wheat, corn, oats, barley, rice, rye, and sugarcane are all grasses. The cattle that produce our beef feed on range grasses. Then they are fattened on grains, such as corn, which are the seeds of grasses. Pigs and chickens are also fed grains to make them grow quickly.

Grasses are specially adapted for dry environments. Their long, slender leaves have little surface area for losing water. Their roots may reach twice as deeply into the ground as their leaves stretch upward, gathering water from deep within the soil. The roots also store energy to help the grass grow after it has been burned, grazed, or mowed.

The roots of these grasses extend deep into the earth.

Some grasses grow in bunches, while others send out shoots in all directions so they cover the ground more evenly.

Prairie grasses come in two types. Cool-season grasses grow best during the cool weather of spring and fall. Others, called warm-season grasses, thrive during the hot, dry summer. Both kinds are mixed together on the prairie, so there is grass growing for grazing animals to eat, whatever the weather.

Many other kinds of plants besides grasses grow on the prairie. They are called *forbs*. Annuals live for only a year. After surviving the winter as seeds, annuals grow quickly during the wet spring. Before dryness sets in, annuals have already bloomed and set seed. Biennials live for two years. The first year, they grow quickly and produce a strong root system as well as a crown of leaves. The biennial survives the winter as roots and a small bunch of leaves close to the ground. The second year, the plant sends up its flowers, sets seed, and dies.

Perennials can live for anywhere from a few years to decades. They develop a strong root system that, along with a few leaves, survives the winter. Most perennials have a long, branched taproot that reaches deep within the soil instead of a thick mat of roots, like grass. Their leaves are usually tough and leathery, to protect them from drying out.

Most forbs belong to either of two plant families, the pea family or the daisy family. Even though they are scattered and present in small numbers, forbs catch our eye with their beautiful flowers. Bright bluish-purple lupine and rose-colored owl clover are both common members of the pea family. Yellow sunflowers, purple or pink asters, and brilliant orange hawkweed are some of the striking daisy family members that thrive on the prairie.

Leadplant, a member of the pea family, is a common prairie plant. Its four-foot roots allow it to grow on dry prairies.

Purple prairie clover is a nutritious plant for animals. It tends to disappear when cattle overgraze the land.

Coneflowers are common prairie wildflowers from the daisy family.

The bur oak is adapted to dryness in a number of ways. The broad spread of its branches helps shade its roots.

Trees are also part of the prairie. They grow along streams and rivers and sometimes even among the tallgrasses. Cottonwood, elm, ash, and box elder line the riverbanks, while bur oaks can sometimes put down their roots among the grasses. The bur oak is especially adapted to life in a dry climate. Its wide, spreading crown of leaves shades its roots, helping keep the ground under the tree from drying out. When a bur oak seed sprouts, it sends down a taproot as long as four feet its very first year, giving it a source of water even during dry spells. Its corky bark protects the trunk and branches from fire, and its leathery leaves reduce water loss.

CHAPTER THREE

Animals of the Prairie

Bison and prairie dogs are probably the most familiar prairie animals. But the prairie is home to thousands of animal species, including insects, spiders, birds, snakes, and many other creatures. Like the plants, prairie animals must be able to tolerate dryness. For spiders and insects, this is easy—they live down among the moist grass stalks, protected from the drying wind. Many larger animals solve the problem of dryness and heat by burrowing.

Insects such as this beetle can retreat from the heat and dryness of the prairie by climbing down among the plants, where it is cooler and more moist.

Prairie dogs are social animals that live in large colonies called towns.

Prairie dogs are well-known burrowers. They live in large colonies or towns, which once stretched for miles across the prairie. The burrows of prairie dogs provide homes for many other animals, such as the burrowing owl and the prairie rattlesnake. The rare black-footed ferret lives in the burrows and feeds largely on the prairie dogs.

This black-footed ferret, emerging from a burrow, is an endangered species. It feeds largely on prairie dogs.

Burrows make good homes for a number of reasons. The air in a burrow is humid, which helps keep animals from losing water from their bodies. While the summer air temperature may range from 77 to 99 degrees Fahrenheit (25 to 37 degrees Celsius), the temperature within a prairie dog burrow varies only from 80 to 89 degrees Fahrenheit (27 to 32 degrees Celsius). And during winter, it's a warm 42 degrees (18 degrees Celsius) inside the burrow when it's 25 (−4 degrees Celsius) outside. The burrow also protects its inhabitants from the drying wind and from fire.

On a prairie, there's no place for a large animal to hide. So it's no surprise that many prairie animals are fast runners. The swift fox lives up to its name by running at 25 miles (40 kilometers) per hour. A coyote can dash after its prey at 40 miles (64 kilometers) per hour. The fastest land animal in North America, the pronghorn, is a prairie dweller. The pronghorn can speed along at 70 miles (113 kilometers) per hour. Even though many prairie birds, such as quail and grouse, can fly, they can also run fast to escape predators.

The pronghorn is a swift prairie resident.

The American bison is a symbol of the prairie. Before European settlers arrived, bison roamed in huge herds containing millions of animals. But within a few decades during the 1800s, bison were reduced to only a few hundred animals, mostly in private herds.

By 1832, no bison lived east of the Mississippi River. By 1900, only twenty wild bison remained in the United States, hiding out in the back country of Yellowstone National Park. Bison were also slaughtered in Canada, so that only about 250 were left in the Canadian wilds by the turn of the century. Fortunately, conservationists and private breeders banded together to bring back the bison. Today, thousands can be found roaming on ranches or in the wild in parts of the United States and Canada.

The animals of the prairie live in harmony with one another. Both prairie dogs and bison eat grass. Yet bison prefer grazing over prairie dog towns, where the grass is short, instead of on other parts of the prairie. Grass that is kept clipped short is more nourishing than tall grass. The constant clipping by the prairie dogs and the bison keeps the grasses in a stage of growth that makes them high in nitrogen, an especially important nutrient. Grass that grows tall and matures has much less nitrogen, so it is less nourishing.

Bison were almost eliminated during the nineteenth century.

Other animals besides bison thrive in prairie dog towns. Like the bison, pronghorn like to feed there. They prefer to eat forbs rather than grasses, and many forbs thrive in the towns. The prairie dogs keep them clipped, so they have a high nitrogen content, just like the grasses. Forty percent of western prairie animals live in prairie dog towns.

Prairie dogs provide food for many predators, too. Swift foxes, red foxes, and black-footed ferrets feed on prairie dogs and other small dog-town residents. Birds such as lark buntings, mountain plovers, and Cassin's sparrows also prefer living in dog towns.

A prairie dog sounds a warning of danger before retreating into its burrow.

The song of the meadowlark adds beauty to the prairie.

CHAPTER FOUR

The Destruction of the Prairie

When Major Stephen H. Long saw the seemingly endless expanse of grass that made up the Central Plains, he called it the Great American Desert. Prairie is not desert. But the name said something about people's attitude toward the prairie. It was a land to be crossed, to be endured. People wanted to settle in the fertile, forested west coast.

After the Far West was settled and railroads that crossed the plains had been built, things changed. The Homestead Act of 1862 promised land for anyone who claimed it. Each person could claim 160 acres, build a house, live on and farm the land for five years, and it was his or hers. The only cost was the $10 filing fee.

The Homestead Act was a great success. Between 1860 and 1900, four hundred million acres of prairie were plowed. The number of farms in the young United States went from two million to six million. And as settlement progressed, the wild prairies disappeared.

A sod house and a rain barrel were the minimum requirements of life for the prairie homesteader.

Today, the view from an airplane window of the prairie states and provinces is a patchwork of squared-off farm fields. In the drier west, wheat is the main crop, while corn grows where the tallgrass once waved. The old tallgrass prairie is now called the Corn Belt. Almost all the original natural prairie is gone.

In the United States, tallgrass prairie once covered 142 million acres in fourteen states. Now, less than 10 percent remains, most in small patches on hilly or other land that is difficult to plow. Large areas of tallgrass exist today only in the Flint Hills of Oklahoma and Kansas. Shortgrass prairie has also disappeared. Where wheat won't grow, cattle graze, even on public lands such as National Wildlife Refuges.

When prairie is plowed and farmed, it has clearly been destroyed. But what about cattle? Grazing would seem like a way of using the prairie without destroying it. Unfortunately, this is not so. A natural wild shortgrass prairie might have 250 different kinds of plants. After a prairie becomes cattle pasture, most of the plants disappear until only about forty species survive.

Today, most of the prairie is plowed and planted.

Cattle destroy prairies in a number of ways. While bison are adapted to life on the prairie, cattle are more suited to moister climates. They can eat grass, but they prefer the leafy forbs that grow in larger quantities along creeks. They also like the shade offered by waterside trees. By concentrating along the water, cattle turn the creek shoreline into muddy plantless zones and pollute the water with their dung.

Cattle are grazed where crops can't be grown.

Eventually, overgrazing results in barren ground, where little or nothing grows.

Much of the grasslands where cattle graze belong to the federal government. They are leased to ranchers. The ranchers are supposed to put only a certain number of cattle onto the land. But often, they allow too many cattle to graze. The cattle eat almost all the forbs and also overgraze the grass, leaving barren areas that can turn to dust. The wind blows away the dust, removing the fertile topsoil and making it difficult for the prairie to recover from the overgrazing.

CHAPTER FIVE

Bringing Back the Prairie

In the past, governments set up parks and preserves to save landscapes that pleased the human eye and spirit. People love to look at mountains, and they are amazed by geysers and giant waterfalls. No one thought about saving the prairie, which seemed empty and lonely. But now that prairies have almost disappeared, people are beginning to value them. Scattered across the plains states, pieces of prairie are being preserved and restored.

Some preserves are small. The 610-acre Willa Cather Memorial Prairie in Nebraska is a gentle monument to Willa Cather, author of novels about the life of prairie pioneers. Such small preserves dot the prairie landscape.

People who spent their lives on the prairie, such as author Willa Cather, came to love it. This bit of prairie in Nebraska is preserved in her name.

A few patches of original prairie still survive.

In Iowa, the U.S. Fish and Wildlife Service is helping to restore an area of former prairie to its original beauty and wildness. Since the land has been grazed, plowed, and built on, the job is very difficult. Seeds must be found for prairie plants. And not just any plants, but those that once grew in this area. Fortunately, bits and pieces of prairie still survive across the plains in isolated spots such as the edges of cemeteries and along railroad rights-of-way. Those who restore the prairie hunt for such remnants and gather seeds for the future there. The goal of the Iowa project, called the Walnut Creek Preserve, is to restore more than 8,000 acres of prairie to their original state.

Wisconsin has several prairie preserves. The University of Wisconsin has restored some prairie land. The Wisconsin chapter of the Nature Conservancy protects a few patches of prairie, including an old railroad right-of-way a half mile (.8 kilometer) long and only 82½ (25 meters) feet wide.

Omro Prairie in Wisconsin is a narrow stretch of original prairie along a railroad right-of-way.

The Tallgrass Prairie Preserve in Oklahoma is an even more ambitious effort to preserve the prairie. The Nature Conservancy, which owns the preserve, plans on expanding it from the original 30,000 acres of ranchland purchased in 1989. As the years go by, the Conservancy intends to recreate the original tallgrass prairie, using bison and fire. At present, the bison herd is too small to graze the whole preserve, so a carefully regulated herd of cattle also grazes there. But with time, 1,800 bison will roam free on the preserve, just as they did before Europeans settled the land. Visitors will be able to stand in one spot and look out over the landscape dotted by the dark bodies of bison. They will enjoy the abundant wildflowers, and they will watch the grass flow wildly in the wind as it once did all across the land. And as more and more prairie land is restored and preserved, visitors in many areas will be able to experience its beauty.

Fires are set to help keep trees from taking over prairies. Most of these trees on the Tallgrass Prairie Preserve in Oklahoma were killed by fire.

Glossary

cool-season grasses   grasses that grow during spring and fall

forbs   leafy plants, often in the daisy or pea family, that live among prairie grasses

grains   the seeds of grasses, such as wheat and corn

mixed-grass prairie   the part of the prairie that falls between the western and eastern prairie. Both shortgrasses and tallgrasses grow here, as well as other grasses 2 to 4 feet (61 to 122 centimeters) tall

shortgrass prairie   the western, dry prairie, where grasses up to 2 feet (61 centimeters) tall grow

tallgrass prairie   the eastern, moist prairie where grasses grow to more than 5 feet (152 centimeters) tall

warm-season grasses   grasses that grow during the summer

Index

(numbers in italics indicate pages with photos)

animals, *11*, *15*, *18*, *20–27*, 30
annuals, 16

bison or buffalo, *11*, *20*, 24, *25*, *26*, 32, 38
bur oak, *19*

Canada, 5, 7, 24
Cather, Willa, 34, *35*
cattle, *18*, 30, *32*, *33*
cool-season grasses, *15*

daisy family, 16, *18*

farms/farming, 28, *29*, 30, *31*, 36
fire, *10*, *11*, *19*, 38
flowers, 16, *18*, *38*
forbs, 16, *26*, *32*, *33*

grains, *13*, *14*, 30

Homestead Act of 1862, The, 28, *29*

Mexico, 5, 7
mixed-grass prairie, *9*, 12

Nature Conservancy, The, *37*, *38*

pea family, 16
perennials, 16
plants, 12–*19*, *20*, *26*, 30, *32*, *33*, 36
prairie dogs, *20*, *21*, *22*, 24, *26*
preservation, 34–*38*

shortgrass prairie, *9*, 12, 30

tallgrass prairie, *9*, 12, *13*, *19*, 30, 38
trees, *19*

warm-season grasses, *15*
weather, *8*, *9*, *10*, 19, *20*, *22*